THE FRAUDULENT TRANSFER HANDBOOK- 1st *Supplement*
A Practical Guide For Lawyers and Clients

By Earl M. Forte

THE FRAUDULENT TRANSFER HANDBOOK – 1ST SUPPLEMENT

by

Earl M. Forte

THE FRAUDULENT TRANSFER HANDBOOK – 1st
Supplement - A PRACTICAL GUIDE FOR LAWYERS
AND CLIENTS
Copyright © 2017 by Earl M. Forte

This is a work of non-fiction.

All rights reserved. No part of this publication may be reproduced, stored in a retrieval system, or transmitted in any form or by any means without the prior written permission of the author, nor be otherwise circulated in any form of binding or cover other than that in which it is published.

To my parents

Preface

In 2017, I re-issued the *Fraudulent Transfer Handbook*, which I originally published in 2013. That book was intended to be used as a reference source for prosecuting and defending fraudulent transfer cases. This first supplement, originally published in 2014, adds to the effort by addressing recent developments in fraudulent transfer case law and adding discussion to several subjects previously covered in the original 2013 edition.

Chapter summaries for 1st supplement

1. The Supreme Court of the U.S., in a fraudulent transfer case, again sets constitutional limits on the powers of bankruptcy judges – *Executive Benefits Insurance Agency v. Arkison*.

Chapter 1 does not supplement a prior chapter in the original *Fraudulent Transfer Handbook,* but rather discusses the much-awaited June 9, 2014, opinion of the Supreme Court of the United States in *Executive Benefits Insurance Agency v. Peter H. Arkison, Chapter 7 Trustee of the Estate of Bellingham Insurance Agency, Inc.*, in which the Court clarified its June 2011 opinion in *Stern v. Marshall,* by again holding that bankruptcy judges lack authority under Article III of the Constitution to enter final judgments and orders on certain types of claims, including the fraudulent transfer claims at issue in the case, even though the claims may be designated as "core" bankruptcy matters in § 157 of the Judiciary Act (so-called "*Stern* claims"). Responding to a practical problem created by *Stern*, the Court also held that when "*Stern* claims" are presented to a bankruptcy judge, the bankruptcy judge may hear them, but must submit proposed findings of fact and conclusions of law to the district court for *de novo* review and entry of final judgment. The Court concluded that because the district court in the case had in fact conducted a *de novo* review of the bankruptcy judge's decision, constitutional requirements under *Stern* had been met and therefore affirmed the lower court decision. The Court did not decide whether bankruptcy judges can exercise Article III judicial powers based on the consent of the parties, leaving that issue "for another day."

2. **What it means to "hinder" or "delay" creditors – *Tronox v. Kerr-McGee*.**

This chapter supplements Chapter 6 in the original *Fraudulent Transfer Handbook* (2013 Ed.) ("'Constructive' vs. 'intentional' fraudulent transfers"), with a discussion of the December 12, 2013, decision of the United States Bankruptcy Court for the Southern District of New York in *Tronox v. Kerr-McGee*. The opinion is helpful in its attention to acts by the debtor that simply "hinder" or "delay" creditors, rather than "defraud" them.

3. **No D&O insurance coverage for fraudulent transfer claims – *Orchard Brands TopCo, LLC v. Twin Cities Fire Insurance Co.*, a case that appears to contradict U.S. Supreme Court precedent.**

This chapter supplements Chapter 19 in the original *Fraudulent Transfer Handbook* (2013 Ed.)("Is there directors and officers liability insurance coverage?") by reviewing the Superior Court of California's decision of January 24, 2014 in *Orchard Brands Topco, LLC v. Twin Cities Fire Insurance Co.,* in which the court held that because a fraudulent transfer claim seeks restitution or disgorgement of wrongfully transferred property, the repayment of a fraudulent transfer by a defendant does not constitute an insurable "loss" under a directors' and officers' liability insurance policy. The opinion appears to ignore prior decisions in the underlying litigation by the federal district court in Delaware and to contradict precedent from the Supreme Court of the United States holding that fraudulent transfer claims brought to recover cash transfers, constitute legal claims for money damages, not equitable claims for restitution.

4. **Tax payments made by the debtor to the IRS, cannot be recovered as fraudulent transfers.**

Chapter 4 does not supplement a prior chapter in the original *Fraudulent Transfer Handbook* (2013 Ed.). Rather, it delves into a new area by reviewing a fraudulent transfer case of first impression for a United States Circuit Court of Appeals, *In re Equipment Acquisition Resources, Inc.*, in which the United States Court of Appeals for the Seventh Circuit held that a bankruptcy trustee did not have a viable claim under the Illinois Uniform Fraudulent Transfer Act to recover tax payments made by the debtor to the IRS.

5. **Calculating statute of limitations tolling periods in state law fraudulent transfer actions.**

Chapter 5 supplements Chapter 10 in the original *Fraudulent Transfer Handbook* (2013 Ed.) ("Reach back and limitations periods") with an exciting (humor) discussion on statutes of limitations for state law claims for intentional fraudulent transfers, the doctrine of equitable tolling and how to calculate the equitable tolling period.

6. **More on the bar against constructive fraudulent transfer claims in § 546(e) of the Bankruptcy Code –** *Tronox v. Kerr-McGee.*

Chapter 6 supplements Chapter 17 in the original *Fraudulent Transfer Handbook* (2013 Ed.) ("The bar against constructive fraudulent transfer claims in § 546(e) of the Bankruptcy Code") with a discussion of the decision by the United States Bankruptcy Court for the Southern District of New York in *Tronox v. Kerr-McGee,* in which the court outlined the requirements for successfully asserting a § 546(e) defense and concluded that the defense was not available to the defendants in that case.

CONTENTS
Page

Preface 1

Chapter summaries for 1st supplement 2

1. The Supreme Court of the U.S., in a fraudulent transfer case, again sets constitutional limits on the powers of bankruptcy judges – *Executive Benefits Insurance Agency v. Arkison* 8

2. What it means to "hinder" or "delay" creditors – *Tronox v. Kerr-McGee.* 19

3. No D&O insurance coverage for fraudulent transfer claims – *Orchard Brands TopCo, LLC v. Twin Cities Fire Insurance Co.*, a case that appears to contradict U.S. Supreme Court precedent 24

4. Tax payments made by the debtor to the IRS, cannot be recovered as fraudulent transfers 34

5. Calculating statute of limitations tolling periods in state law fraudulent transfer actions 37

6. More on the bar against constructive fraudulent transfer claims in § 546(e) of the Bankruptcy Code – *Tronox v. Kerr-McGee* 43

Table of authorities 48

Index 53

About the author 57

1.

The Supreme Court of the U.S., in a fraudulent transfer case, again sets constitutional limits on the powers of bankruptcy judges – *Executive Benefits Insurance Agency v. Arkison.*

On June 9, 2014, the Supreme Court of the United States delivered its much-awaited opinion in the fraudulent transfer case of *Executive Benefits Insurance Agency, Petitioner v. Peter H. Arkison, Chapter 7 Trustee of the Estate of Bellingham Insurance Agency, Inc.*, 573 U.S. ___, 2014 WL 2560461 (2014) ("*Executive Benefits*"). The unanimous decision confirms the Court's prior opinion in *Stern v. Marshall*, 131 S. Ct. 2594 (2011) ("*Stern*"), which caused a national stir by setting broad constitutional limits on the powers of bankruptcy judges to enter final judgments and orders on certain types of claims, even if those claims are designated as "core" bankruptcy matters in § 157 of Title 28 of the United States Code (the "Judiciary Act"). The opinion in *Executive Benefits* notes the importance of the two characteristics required for exercise of the federal judicial power set forth in Article III of the Constitution (life tenure and no diminution in pay by Congress) and emphasizes how the absence of these two characteristics in bankruptcy judges bars them from adjudicating certain types of claims. The opinion builds on the Court's prior decisions in *Northern Pipeline Construction Co. v. Marathon Pipe Line Co.*, 458 U.S. 50 (1984) ("*Northern Pipeline*") and *Granfinanciera, S.A. v. Nordberg*, 492 U.S. 33 (1989) ("*Granfinanciera*"), which both raised the issue of constitutional limits on the power of bankruptcy judges due to their lack of life tenure and salary protection. In *Executive Benefits*, the Court also solved a practical problem created by *Stern*, by instructing that bankruptcy judges should handle "*Stern* claims" in the same way they handle "non-core" claims.

An issue not decided by the Supreme Court in *Executive Benefits*, which had been a major issue in the lower court proceedings, was whether bankruptcy judges can exercise Article III judicial powers based on the consent of the parties. The Court left that issue "for another day."

Executive Benefits Insurance Agency, 573 U.S. __ at 4, n. 4, 2014 WL 2560461 at *4, n. 4.

The relevant facts and procedural background of *Executive Benefits* were as follows: the Executive Benefits Insurance Agency ("EBIA") was sued by a bankruptcy trustee on a fraudulent transfer claim in the United States Bankruptcy Court for the Western District of Washington. The bankruptcy judge granted summary judgment in favor of the trustee and against EBIA and EBIA appealed to the district court, which affirmed. EBIA then appealed further to the United States Court of Appeals for the Ninth Circuit. *Id.* at 2, *3.

In the Ninth Circuit, EBIA argued for reversal of the district court's decision on the ground that under *Stern* and other case law the bankruptcy court lacked power to enter final judgment and EBIA was entitled to a trial in the district court as a matter of law. *Executive Benefits Insurance Agency v. Arkison (In the Matter of Bellingham Insurance Agency, Inc.),* 702 F. 3d 553, 557 (9th Cir. 2012).

Relying on *Northern Pipeline, Granfinanciera, Stern* and other cases, the Ninth Circuit held that because bankruptcy judges are appointed by the Circuit Courts of Appeal for non-life terms of 14 years and have salaries subject to diminution by Congress, EBIA was correct in arguing that bankruptcy judges cannot exercise "[t]he judicial Power of the United States." *Executive Benefits Insurance Agency v. Arkison*, 702 F. 3d at 558 *citing* 28 U.S.C. §§ 152(a)(1), 153(a) and U.S. Const. art. III, § 1. This was so, the Ninth Circuit reasoned, even though the Judiciary Act designates certain claims, such as the fraudulent transfer claims brought against EBIA, as "core" bankruptcy matters that may be adjudicated by a bankruptcy judge. *Id.* at 564. When such claims are presented (referred to as "*Stern* claims"), bankruptcy judges may hear the claims, but must submit proposed findings of fact and conclusions of law to the district court for *de novo* review and entry of final judgment. *Id.* at 565-66.[1]

Although the Ninth Circuit agreed with EBIA that the bankruptcy judge was constitutionally barred from entering final judgment against EBIA, its ultimate decision was of no benefit to EBIA, because it also found that on the facts presented, EBIA had "consented" to entry of final judgment by the bankruptcy judge because it had failed to raise the constitutional issue in the lower court proceedings, waiting

---

[1] As the Ninth Circuit noted, "[a] majority of the *Northern Pipeline* court also acknowledged that it is constitutionally permissible for an Article III court to assign fact finding responsibility to an adjunct, provided that the Article III court retains 'the essential attributes of the judicial power.' Nevertheless, the Supreme Court has determined that the bankruptcy court is not an 'adjunct' of either the district court or the Court of Appeals." *Executive Benefits Insurance Agency*, 702 F. 3d at 559, n. 4.

until shortly before oral argument in the Ninth Circuit to do so, thereby waiving its right to a trial in the district court. While EBIA conceded that it had not raised the constitutional issue in the bankruptcy court or in its first appeal to the district court, it argued that under *Stern* the bankruptcy court still lacked constitutional authority to enter final judgment. *Executive Benefits Insurance Agency*, 702 F. 3d at 557. EBIA further argued that it had raised the constitutional issue timely in the Ninth Circuit by moving to vacate the bankruptcy court's judgment shortly after the Supreme Court delivered its opinion in *Stern* on June 23, 2011. *Id.* at 556, 569.

The Ninth Circuit disagreed with EBIA on the consent/waiver issue, noting that EBIA had failed to raise the constitutional issue in the bankruptcy court and in the district court despite the existence of decisions such as *Northern Pipeline*, *Granfinanciera* and the Ninth Circuit's prior decision in *Marshall v. Stern*, 600 F. 3d 1037 (9th Cir. 2010), which all pre-dated *Stern* and which all raised the issue of constitutional limits on the power of bankruptcy judges to decide certain claims due to their lack of life tenure and salary protection. [2] *Executive Benefits Insurance*

---

[2] The Ninth Circuit also noted that EBIA had engaged in procedural gamesmanship on the "consent" issue by making a jury demand in the bankruptcy court, seeking a jury trial in the district court by moving to

Agency v. Arkison, 702 F. 3d at 556-59, 566-70. Thus, the Ninth Circuit ruled against EBIA and affirmed the bankruptcy court's decision, based largely on its conclusion that EBIA had waived its right to a trial in the district court by implicitly consenting to entry of final judgment by the bankruptcy judge.

On certiorari, the Supreme Court agreed with the Ninth Circuit (and with EBIA) on the constitutional issue, concluding, as it had in *Stern*, that while bankruptcy judges are statutorily empowered by § 157 of the Judiciary Act to adjudicate all "core" bankruptcy matters, including fraudulent transfer claims, they are constitutionally barred from doing so with respect to certain types of "core" bankruptcy matters because they lack life tenure and salary protection. *Executive Benefits*, 573 U.S. ___ at 1, 5, 2014 WL 2560461 at * 3, * 5. The Supreme Court acknowledged the dilemma its decision in *Stern* had created for bankruptcy judges, i.e., while the Judiciary Act provides that for non-core claims, a bankruptcy judge can hear the claims but must submit proposed findings of fact and conclusions of law to

---

withdraw the bankruptcy reference, and then petitioning the district court to stay that motion in order "to give the bankruptcy judge an opportunity to adjudicate the [fraudulent transfer] claim." *Executive Benefits Insurance Agency v. Arkison*, 702 F. 3d at 568. These maneuvers by EBIA clearly undermined its position before the Ninth Circuit on the issue of whether it had consented to entry of final judgment by the bankruptcy judge.

the district court for *de novo* review and entry of judgment, it makes no similar provision for "core" bankruptcy matters that cannot be heard by the bankruptcy judge for constitutional reasons. How then are bankruptcy judges to handle these so-called "*Stern* claims," i.e., claims that are designated as "core" bankruptcy matters in § 157 of the Judiciary Act, but which bankruptcy judges are constitutionally barred from adjudicating? *Id.* at 4, * 4.

The Supreme Court devised a practical solution to this problem. It began by first asking whether a bankruptcy judge could simply treat a core "*Stern* claim" as if it were "non-core" and hear the case but submit proposed findings of fact and conclusions of law to the district court for *de novo* review and entry of final judgment? *Id.* at 9, *7.

Relying on the separability provision in the 1984 bankruptcy amendments to the Judiciary Act, where the core/non-core designation was created, the Court concluded that "*Stern* claims" (core bankruptcy matters that cannot be decided by a bankruptcy judge for constitutional reasons), can be treated as if they were non-core claims and made subject to the requirement that bankruptcy judges submit proposed findings of fact and conclusions of law to the district court for *de novo* review and entry of final judgment. *Executive Benefits*, 573 U.S. ___ at 9-10, 2014 WL 2560461 at

*7 - *8. The separability provision from the 1984 bankruptcy amendments that the Supreme Court relied upon to support this result states:

> If any provision of this Act...or the application thereof to any person or circumstance is held invalid, the remainder of this Act, or the application of that provision to persons or circumstances other than those as to which it is held invalid, is not affected thereby.

See Note following 28 U.S.C. § 151; *Executive Benefits*, 573 U.S. at 9-10, 2014 WL 2560461 at *7. Based on this provision, the Supreme Court reasoned that simply because it had found portions of 28 U.S.C. § 157 to be unconstitutional by improperly conferring the federal judicial power on bankruptcy judges who lack life tenure and salary protection, the other parts of the statute remain in full force and effect and it would not violate the core/non-core distinction in the statute for bankruptcy judges to treat "*Stern* claims" as if they were non-core claims subject to *de novo* review in the district court. The Supreme Court wrote:

> The bankruptcy court should hear the proceeding [*i.e.*, the *Stern* claim], and submit proposed findings of fact and conclusions of law to the district court for *de novo* review and entry of judgment.

Executive Benefits, 573 U.S. ___ at 10, 2014 WL 2560461 at *7.

While the Supreme Court's decision in *Executive Benefits* solved a practical problem for the nation's bankruptcy courts by instructing that "*Stern* claims" should be handled in the same way as non-core claims and submitted to the district court for *de novo* review and entry of final judgment, its decision was of no help to EBIA, because it further observed that this is exactly what had happened in the case before it: "[b]ecause the District Court in this case conducted the *de novo* review that the petitioner [EBIA] demands, we affirm the judgment of the Court of Appeals upholding the District Court's decision." *Id.* at 1, * 3.

A significant issue *not* decided by the Supreme Court in *Executive Benefits*, which had been a major issue in the lower court proceedings, was whether bankruptcy judges can exercise Article III judicial powers and enter final judgments on "*Stern* claims" based on the consent of the parties and whether such consent had implicitly been given by EBIA based on its failure to timely raise the constitutional issue. The Supreme Court side-stepped this question, reasoning that because it had already concluded that the district court had complied with constitutional requirements by conducting a *de novo* review of the bankruptcy court's decision, "this case does not require us to address whether

EBIA in fact consented to the Bankruptcy Court's adjudication of a *Stern* claim and whether Article III permits a bankruptcy court, with the consent of the parties, to enter final judgment on a *Stern* claim. We reserve that question for another day." *Id.* at 4, n. 4, * 4, n. 4.

Thus, while *Executive Benefits* confirms *Stern* and prior Supreme Court precedent setting constitutional limits on the powers of bankruptcy judges, and also solves the practical problem of how bankruptcy judges should handle *Stern* claims, it does not address the issue of whether Article III judicial powers can be conferred on bankruptcy judges by consent of the parties.

Bankruptcy judges will likely react to the *Executive Benefits* decision by submitting proposed findings of fact and conclusions of law to the district court for *de novo* review in any case where their constitutional authority to adjudicate certain claims could possibly be challenged on appeal. Practitioners should take note and conform to the new regime by submitting proposed findings of fact and conclusions of law to the bankruptcy judge at the time of trial whenever required. This obviously will create some additional work for trial counsel and will result in some delay while the district court conducts its *de novo* review. However, it should save substantial time in the appeal process by eliminating the first level of appeal to the district court, by allowing the parties to appeal directly to the Circuit Court of Appeals following entry of final judgment by the district court. *See generally* Fed. R. App. Pro. 6.

2.

What it means to "hinder" or "delay" creditors – *Tronox v. Kerr-McGee.*

As discussed in the original *Fraudulent Transfer Handbook* (2013 Ed.), because actual intent to defraud creditors is difficult to prove with direct evidence, the Uniform Fraudulent Transfer Act ("UFTA"), the Uniform Fraudulent Conveyance Act ("UFCA") and § 548 of the United States Bankruptcy Code, 11 U.S. C. § 101, *et seq.* (the "Bankruptcy Code"), permit the plaintiff to prove actual intent through circumstantial evidence, so-called "badges of fraud," which are factual scenarios or conduct by the debtor from which actual intent to defraud creditors can be inferred. State versions of the UFTA typically contain a non-exclusive list of examples of "badges of fraud." Additional "badges of fraud" have developed through case law. Essentially, any conduct from which a reasonable inference can be drawn that the debtor intended to defraud creditors, can constitute a "badge of fraud." *E.g.*, 6 Del. C. § 1304(b) (2011); Cal. Civ. Code § 3429.04(b) (2011); 12 Pa. C.S. § 5104(b); Annoted Laws of Massachusetts ("ALM") GL Ch. 109A, § 5(b) (2010). Most courts require a plaintiff to prove "badges of fraud" by clear and convincing evidence. *See* Forte, Earl M., *The Fraudulent Transfer Handbook* (2013 Ed.) at 39-41, n. 11.

But can "actual intent" be proven by showing that the debtor engaged in acts that merely "hindered" or "delayed" creditors in their collection efforts, i.e., can a plaintiff meet its burden of proving "actual intent" by presenting evidence of hindrance and delay alone, or must more heinous "badges of fraud" be proven?

In *Tronox, Inc., et al. v. Kerr-McGee Corp., et al.*, 503 B.R. 239, 277-282 (Bankr. S.D.N.Y. 2013) ("*Tronox*"), the United States Bankruptcy Court for the Southern District of New York, in a lengthy opinion, answered "yes" to this question, holding that a plaintiff bringing a claim to recover intentional fraudulent transfers can satisfy the "actual intent" requirement by showing that the debtor engaged in acts that simply hindered or delayed creditors, i.e., that proving more heinous "badges of fraud" is not required by § 548(a)(1)(A) of the Bankruptcy Code or the UFTA. *Id.*

Tronox involved fraudulent transfer and other claims brought by the trustee of a litigation trust created by the debtor's chapter 11 plan of reorganization. The trustee brought the claims against the Kerr-McGee Corporation and certain of its affiliates, which included claims for intentional fraudulent transfers under § 548 of the Bankruptcy Code and the Oklahoma UFTA. *See* 11 U.S.C. § 548. The claims sought to avoid the transfer of large swaths of Kerr-McGee's assets, made as part of a strategic plan devised by Kerr-McGee to shelter its most valuable assets from large legacy environmental and tort liabilities. *Id.* at 280. The bankruptcy court determined that this activity by Kerr-McGee "hindered" and "delayed" the legacy tort creditors - "In the present case, there can be no dispute that Kerr-McGee acted to free substantially all its assets – certainly its most valuable assets – from 85 years of environmental and tort liabilities. The obvious consequence of this act was that the legacy creditors would not be able to claim against 'substantially all of the Kerr-McGee assets,' and with a minimal asset base against which to recover in the future, would accordingly be 'hindered and delayed' as the direct consequence of the scheme." *Id.* In reaching this conclusion, the court distinguished between acts of fraud and acts of delay or hindrance. The court wrote:

> The intent to defraud is something distinct from the mere intent to delay or hinder. *In re Braus*, 248 F. 55, 64 (2d Cir. 1917) (citation omitted); *see also, In re Duncan & Forbes Dev., Inc.*, 368 B.R. 27, 34 (Bankr. C.D. Cal. 2006). Liability is imposed for "intentional fraudulent conveyance" where the fact and purpose of a conveyance may have been known to creditors in whole or in part, but the transferor intended to hinder or delay them. As the Supreme Court stated in *Shapiro v. Wilgus*, 287 U.S. 348, 354, 53 S.Ct. 142, 77 L.Ed. 355 (1932), "A conveyance is illegal if made with an intent to hinder and delay them."

Id. at 278. Applying this and other legal principles to the facts presented (facts that described the plan devised by Kerr-McGee management and its bankers to protect the company's most valuable assets by isolating its legacy environmental and tort liabilities in the chapter 11 debtors), the court in *Tronox* concluded "that Plaintiffs established by clear and convincing evidence that Defendants intended to hinder and delay the legacy creditors." *Id.* at 250-60, 284. The court also found the presence of numerous "badges of fraud." *Id.* at 282-85.[3]

The *Tronox* case is unusual, but also very helpful, in its attention to the "hinder" and "delay" language in § 548 of

---

[3] The *Tronox* litigation settled in April 2014 after trial for $5.15 billion. *See Anadarko Petroleum Settles U.S.-Wide Clean-Up Case For $5.15 Billion*, Reuters, April 3, 2014.

the Bankruptcy Code and the UFTA. It is a reminder that clear and convincing evidence of acts by the debtor that simply "hinder" or "delay" creditors, not necessarily "defraud" them, is sufficient to prove actual intent for an intentional fraudulent transfer claim. In most cases, presenting evidence of mere hindrance or delay will be easier for the plaintiff than proving "badges of fraud", since any transfer of the debtor's assets made during the applicable limitations period that has the effect of slowing down creditors in their collection efforts or that makes fewer assets available for collection, could conceivably be sufficient to prove "actual intent."

3.

No D&O insurance coverage for fraudulent transfer claims – *Orchard Brands TopCo, LLC v. Twin Cities Fire Insurance Co.*, a case that appears to contradict U.S. Supreme Court precedent.

Chapter 19 of the original *Fraudulent Transfer Handbook* (2013 Ed.) discussed the availability of directors and officers ("D&O") liability insurance coverage for defendants in fraudulent transfer actions. Based on a number of theories that insurance carriers may rely upon, Chapter 19 concluded that D&O insurance coverage is often not made available to defendants in fraudulent transfer cases, either to pay judgments, settlements or defense costs. *See* Forte, Earl M., *The Fraudulent Transfer Handbook* (2013 Ed.) at 107-110.

The issue of D&O liability insurance coverage in fraudulent transfer cases was addressed in January 2014, by the Superior Court for the County of San Francisco, California, in *Orchard Brands TopCo, LLC, et al. v. Twin Cities Fire Insurance Company, et al.*, Case No. CGC-12-526950, Statement of Decision – Phase I, Bifurcated Trial (January 24, 2014) (*"Orchard Brands"*).

In *Orchard Brands* the plaintiffs, Orchard Brands TopCo, LLC ("Orchard Brands") and Golden Gate Private Equity, Inc. ("Golden Gate"), filed a declaratory judgment action seeking D&O indemnity coverage from Twin Cities Fire Insurance Company ("Twin Cities") and various excess D&O insurance carriers for a $75 million settlement that Golden Gate had agreed to pay to settle fraudulent transfer and other claims in *Michaelson v. Golden Gate Private Equity, Inc., et al.*, Case No. 11-51847 (Bankr. Del. 2011).[4] *See also Michaelson v. Farmer, et al. (In re Appleseed's Intermediate Holdings, LLC)*, 470 B.R. 289 (D. Del. 2012) (jointly, *"Michaelson"* or *"In re Appleseed's Intermediate Holdings, LLC"*). The issues in *Orchards Brands* were bifurcated to first address insurance coverage for the fraudulent transfer claims.

---

[4] The excess carriers in *Orchard Brands* were: Arch Insurance Company; U.S. Specialty Insurance Company; Catlin Specialty Insurance Company; and Great American Insurance Company. *See Orchard Brands* at 1, n.1.

In *Michaelson* (the underlying action in *Orchard Brands*), the trustee of a liquidating trust created by a debtors' chapter 11 plan of reorganization, sued Golden Gate and various affiliated parties to recover corporate dividend payments totaling $310 million. The dividends were paid by the debtors in connection with a $725 million secured loan transaction. Of the $725 million in secured loan proceeds, $310 million had been used to fund the dividends to Golden Gate and the other defendants. *Orchard Brands* at 1-2; *Michaelson v. Farmer*, 470 B. R. at 293.

In his complaint, originally filed in the United States Bankruptcy Court for the District of Delaware, but subsequently transferred to the district court for a jury trial, the liquidating trustee in *Michaelson* alleged that the $310 million in dividend payments constituted intentional and constructive fraudulent transfers under the Delaware UFTA and should be returned to the debtors' estate to pay creditors. *Michaelson v. Farmer*, 470 B.R. at 299. The parties settled the case before trial, with Golden Gate agreeing to pay the trustee $75 million. *Orchard Brands*, at 1. The case before the Superior Court of California in *Orchard Brands*, related solely to the issue of whether D&O liability insurance proceeds were available to cover the $75 million settlement of the trustee's fraudulent transfer claims, i.e., did payment of the $75 million to settle the trustee's fraudulent transfer claims, constitute an insurable "loss" under the debtor's D&O policies? *Id.* at 3.

The Superior Court began its analysis with a review of the trustee's complaint. It also reviewed the definition of the word "loss" in the Twin Cities and excess D&O policies, as well as the policies' loss exclusion provisions, which excluded coverage for a "deliberately fraudulent act or omission or any willful violation of law by an Insured, or their gaining any personal profit, remuneration or advantage to which they were not legally entitled. . .established by any final adjudication." *Id.* at 7-8. The court noted that under the policies, "loss" did not include "matters that are deemed uninsurable under the law pursuant to which this Policy shall be construed." *Id.* at 8.

Next, the court reviewed California insurance law (which governed the D&O policies) on the issue of the insurability of claims that seek to have the insured surrender property "wrongfully" obtained. *Id.* at 9-12. The court concluded that because the fraudulent transfer claims asserted by the trustee in *Michaelson* had sought to have the defendants return the $310 million in dividend payments on the ground that they had never been entitled to receive them, the claims sought "restitution" and "disgorgement" and therefore were not insurable under California law and could not be covered by the Twin Cities or the excess D&O insurance policies. *Orchard Brands* at 11-12. In reaching this conclusion, the court relied on the Seventh Circuit's opinion in *Level 3 Communications, Inc. v. Federal Insurance Company*, 272 F. 3d 908 (7th Cir. 2001) ("*Level 3*") and recited the following language from *Level 3*: "An insured incurs no loss within the meaning of the insurance contract by being compelled to return property that it had stolen, even if a more polite word than 'stolen' is used to characterize the claim for the property's return." *Id.* at 910-11.[5]

The decision in *Orchard Brands* aligns with the Seventh Circuit's opinion in *Level 3* and the Fifth Circuit Court of Appeal's decision in *Stanley v. U.S. Bank, N.A. (In re TransTexas Gas Corp.)*, 597 F. 3d 298, 310-11 (5th Cir. 2010) ("*TransTexas*"), in that all three opinions conclude that cash payments ordered by a court to be returned to a plaintiff on the ground that they constituted fraudulent

---

[5] Use of this quotation from *Level 3* by the Superior Court of California in *Orchard Brands* is curious, given that the federal district court in Delaware determined in the underlying litigation that the $310 million in dividend payments the trustee was seeking to recover as fraudulent transfers, were corporate dividends that had been properly declared and issued by the debtor company. *Michaelson v. Farmer, et al. (In re Appleseed's Intermediate Holdings, LLC, et al.)*, 470 B.R. at 298-99. This finding by the Delaware court hardly suggests that the defendants in *Orchard Brands* received "stolen" property.

transfers, amounts to "disgorgement" of an ill-gotten gain, a form of equitable "restitution" that is not an insurable "loss" under a D&O policy. *See* Forte, Earl M., *The Fraudulent Transfer Handbook* (2013 Ed.), Chapter 19 ("Is there directors and officers liability insurance coverage?") at 107-10.

So, have the courts conclusively determined that fraudulent transfer claims cannot be covered by a D&O liability insurance policy? Not exactly.

As stated in footnote 29 of the original *Fraudulent Transfer Handbook*, the decisions in *Level 3, TransTexas Gas* (and now also *Orchard Brands*) denying D&O insurance coverage for fraudulent transfer claims on the ground that they seek "restitution," appear to be inconsistent with precedent from the Supreme Court of the United States holding that fraudulent transfer claims that seek to recover cash transfers (as did the claims in *Orchard Brands*), constitute legal claims for money damages, not equitable claims for "restitution." *See* Forte, Earl M., *The Fraudulent Transfer Handbook* (2013 Ed.) at 109, n. 29 *citing Granfinanciera, S.A. v. Nordberg*, 492 U.S. at 43-48.

In *Granfinanciera*, perhaps the leading Supreme Court opinion discussing the nature of fraudulent transfer claims, a trustee brought a fraudulent transfer claim in bankruptcy court to recover cash transfers. *Id.* at 37. The defendant, who had not filed a proof of claim in the underlying bankruptcy case, made a jury demand, which was struck by the bankruptcy court on the ground that fraudulent transfer claims are equitable claims that seek restitution to which no jury trial right attaches. The case proceeded to a non-jury trial in the bankruptcy court and judgment was entered in favor of the trustee. On appeal, the district court, and subsequently the United States Court of Appeals for the Eleventh Circuit, affirmed the bankruptcy court on the jury trial issue, ruling that because fraudulent transfer claims are a form of equitable claim that seek restitution, not legal claims for money damages, no jury trial right attached in favor of the defendant. *Id.* at 38.

The Supreme Court granted certiorari and reversed. It concluded, after an extensive analysis, that fraudulent transfer claims that seek to recover cash payments, as did the trustee's claims in *Granfinanciera*, are legal claims for money damages, *not* equitable claims for restitution, and therefore the defendant, who the Supreme Court noted had not filed a proof of claim in the underlying bankruptcy case, was entitled to a jury trial. *Id.* at 46-47, 58. In reaching its decision in *Granfinanciera*, the Supreme Court specifically rejected the argument adopted by the Superior Court of

California in *Orchard Brands*, namely, that a fraudulent transfer claim that seeks to recover cash transfers made by the debtor, constitutes an equitable claim for "restitution." *Id.* at 49 n.7.

The facts and procedural history in *Orchard Brands* are similar to the facts and procedural history in *Granfinanciera* in a key respect – like the defendant in *Granfinanciera*, four of the defendants in *Orchard Brands* who had not filed proofs of claim in the underlying bankruptcy case, demanded a jury trial and, based on *Granfinanciera* and other case law, filed a motion with the district court seeking to withdraw the bankruptcy reference for a jury trial in the district court. The motion was granted and the action proceeded in the district court as a jury case, where it ultimately settled before trial. *Michaelson v. Golden Gate Private Equity, Inc., et al. (In re Appleseed's Intermediate Holdings, LLC)*, 2011 WL 6293251 at * 1-*4 (D. Del. 2011).

Thus, well before the insurance coverage dispute was presented to the Superior Court of California in *Orchard Brands*, the United States District Court for the District of Delaware had determined in the underlying litigation, that the fraudulent transfer claims at issue were legal claims that sought money damages to which the jury trial right attached in favor of four of the defendants. There is no mention of this in the Superior Court of California's decision in *Orchard Brands*, nor does the Superior Court explain the obvious contradiction between its conclusion that the trustee's fraudulent transfer claims were equitable claims that sought "restitution" and the district of Delaware's conclusion that the same claims constituted legal claims for money damages to which the jury trial right attached. If the California Superior Court had applied the reasoning of *Granfinanciera* and ruled consistently with the district of Delaware's prior decisions in the underlying litigation, it may have reached a different conclusion on the issue of insurable "loss."[6]

Practitioners should take note of the defects in *Orchard Brands* and not simply assume that *Orchard Brands*, *Level 3* or *TransTexas Gas* are the final word on the issue of whether a fraudulent transfer claim seeks recovery of an insurable "loss" under a D&O liability insurance policy. If

---

[6] One commentator has suggested that "restitution" can be used as a theory for measuring monetary damages based on the defendant's gain, as opposed to the plaintiff's injury. *See* Rendleman, Doug, *Measurement of Restitution: Coordinating Restitution with Compensatory Damages and Punitive Damages*, 68 Washington & Lee L. Rev. 973 (2011) at 975-76, 991. Even assuming that such an approach would apply to a fraudulent transfer claim, under the Supreme Court's analysis in *Granfinanciera*, a court-ordered repayment of a monetary fraudulent transfer would still constitute a legal claim for money damages. *See Granfinanciera, S.A., et al. v. Nordberg*, 492 U.S. at 41, 48.

a subsequent court takes a closer look, the result could be different.

4.

Tax payments made by the debtor to the IRS, cannot be recovered as fraudulent transfers.

In a case of first impression for a United States Court of Appeals, in *In re Equipment Acquisition Resources, Inc.*, 742 F. 3d 743 (7th Cir. 2014) (*"Equipment Acquisition"*), the Court of Appeals for the Seventh Circuit addressed the issue of whether a bankruptcy trustee could recover as fraudulent transfers under the Illinois UFTA, tax payments that the debtor, a sub-chapter S corporation, had made to the IRS on behalf of its shareholders. The trustee settled with the IRS with respect to eight of the tax payments, but the litigation proceeded with respect to a ninth. *Id.* at 744-45.

Based on the waiver of sovereign immunity of governmental units contained in § 106(a) of the Bankruptcy Code, the bankruptcy court, and subsequently the district court in the first appeal, concluded in *Equipment Acquisitions* that the trustee could bring a fraudulent transfer claim against the IRS to recover the tax payment. *Id.*

However, in the second appeal, the Seventh Circuit reversed, rejecting the trustee's argument that the action was viable based on the waiver of sovereign immunity in § 106 of the Bankruptcy Code. *Equipment Acquisitions,* 742 F. 3d at 746-47. Although the Seventh Circuit agreed that § 106(a)(1) of the Bankruptcy Code contains a waiver of sovereign immunity that generally allowed suits to proceed against the federal government in bankruptcy matters, it said that more was required to determine whether the trustee's fraudulent transfer claim was viable under the Illinois UFTA. The court reviewed the requirements a trustee must satisfy to bring a state law fraudulent transfer claim pursuant to the § 544 "strong arm" power in the Bankruptcy Code and concluded that because Illinois law did not permit an unsecured creditor of the debtor to bring a fraudulent transfer claim to recover the tax payment outside of bankruptcy, a trustee in bankruptcy could not do so either – i.e., the trustee could not satisfy the "actual creditor" requirement of § 544(b) of the Bankruptcy Code by showing that the payment was "voidable under applicable [state] law." *Id.* at 747.

In rendering its decision, the Seventh Circuit acknowledged that its interpretation of the interplay between § 106(a) and § 544(b) of the Bankruptcy Code "diverge[d] from all of the bankruptcy and district courts to consider the issue in the context of the federal government." *Equipment Acquisitions,* 742 F. 3d at 748. However, the Seventh Circuit concluded that other courts that had addressed the issue had "focused too narrowly on the language in § 106(a)(1), and largely disregarded § 544(b)'s actual-creditor requirement." *Id.* at 749. The Seventh Circuit therefore reversed the district court and concluded that the trustee could not recover the debtor's tax payment to the IRS as a fraudulent transfer under the Illinois UFTA. *Id.* at 749.

Time will tell whether other Circuit Courts of Appeal will follow the Seventh Circuit's decision in *Equipment Acquisitions.* The principal point of *Equipment Acquisitions* for practitioners is not to overlook the "actual creditor" requirement in § 544(b)(1) of the Bankruptcy Code when bringing or defending against state law fraudulent transfer claims filed in bankruptcy cases and to take particular care if the transfers at issue were tax payments to the IRS.

5.

Calculating statute of limitations tolling periods in state law fraudulent transfer actions.

Chapter 10 of the original *Fraudulent Transfer Handbook* (2013 Ed.) discussed reach back and limitations periods in fraudulent transfer actions. This supplement to prior Chapter 10, adds further discussion on the subject of state law statutes of limitations, the doctrine of equitable tolling and how to calculate the equitable tolling period.

The UFTA, as adopted in most states, provides that a cause of action for intentional or constructive fraudulent transfers or obligations is extinguished unless it is brought within four years after the transfer was made or obligation incurred. *E.g.*, 6 Del. C. § 1309; Cal. Civ. Code § 3439.09; ALM GL ch. 109A § 10; 12 Pa. C.S. § 5109. Other states have statutes of limitations periods for fraudulent transfer claims that extend further than the typical four years. *E.g.*, Iowa Code Ann. § 684.9 (five years); Kentucky, Ky. Rev. Stat. Ann. § 413.120 (five years); Maine, Me. Rev. Stat. Ann. tit. 14, § 3580 (six years); Michigan, Mich. Comp. Laws Ann. §§ 566.39, 600.5813 (six years); Minnesota, Minn. Stat. Ann. § 541.05 (six years); New York, N.Y. C.P.L.R. §§ 203(g), 213 (8)(six years).

As noted in prior Chapter 10, these statutes of limitations periods are subject to the doctrine of equitable tolling for intentional fraudulent transfers claims, but not for constructive fraudulent transfer claims. *See* Forte, Earl M., *The Fraudulent Transfer Handbook* (2013 Ed.) at 59. The UFTA commonly provides for a one-year equitable tolling period for intentional fraudulent transfers claims, as follows:

> A cause of action with respect to a fraudulent transfer or obligation under this chapter is extinguished unless action is brought:
>
> (1) Under § 1304(a)(1) [intentional fraudulent transfers] of this title, within 4 years after the transfer was made or the obligation was incurred or, if later, *within 1 year after the transfer or obligation was or could reasonably have been discovered by the claimant*;
>
> (2) Under § 1304(a)(2) or § 1305(a) [constructive fraudulent transfers] of this title, within 4 years after the transfer was made or the obligation was incurred;

(emphasis added); 6 Del. C. § 1309; *see also* Cal. Civ. Code § 3439.09; ALM GL ch. 109A § 10; 12 Pa. C.S. § 5109. New York, which has a six-year statute of limitations period for fraudulent transfer claims, provides for a two-year tolling period for intentional fraudulent transfer claims. N.Y. C.P.L.R. §§ 203(g), 213(8); *Childs v. Brandon*, 90 A.D.2d 983, 984 (N.Y. App. Div. 4th Dep't, 1982); *Miller v. Polow, et al.*, 14 A.D.3d 368 (N.Y. App. Div. 2005); *Sargiss v. Magarelli*, 50 A.D. 3d 1117, 1118 (N.Y. App. Div. 2008); *Ehrler v. Cataffo*, 42 A.D. 3d 424 (N.Y. App. Div. 2007).

How is the one (or two) year equitable tolling period calculated for intentional fraudulent transfer claims?

Start by calculating the original statute of limitations period by first identifying the date of the transfer or obligation and counting forward four (or five, or six, as the case may be) years, beginning with the day immediately following the date of the transfer or obligation as "day one". Based on this calculation, if suit was filed later than four (or five, or six) years after the date of the transfer or obligation, next identify the date on which the transfer or obligation was or reasonably could have been discovered by the plaintiff and count one (or two, as the case may be) years forward from that date. Under an equitable tolling analysis, this would mean determining "when the plaintiff is on actual or inquiry notice of the fraud" and may require some level of investigation or fact discovery. *In re Bennett Funding Group, Inc.*, 367 B.R. 302 (Bankr. N.D. N.Y. 2007). "For a plaintiff to be on inquiry notice, he need not be aware of all aspects of the alleged fraud...rather, a plaintiff is on inquiry notice at the time at which the plaintiff should have discovered the general fraudulent scheme." *Id.* And while reasonable diligence is required of a plaintiff to make use of the one or two-year tolling period, "unless it conclusively appears that the plaintiff had knowledge of facts from which the alleged fraud might be reasonably inferred, a claim for fraud should not be barred by the Statute of Limitations." *Lavin v. Kaufman*, 226 A.D. 2d 107, 108-09 (N.Y. App. Div. 1996); *Citicorp Trust Bank, FSB v. Makkar, et al.*, 67 A.D. 3d 950, 953 (N.Y. App. Div. 2d Dept. 2009). The mere fact that a plaintiff "knew something was amiss" or had knowledge of some "injury-in-fact" will not by itself constitute notice of the fraud as a matter of law. *The Government of India and The Food Corporation of India v. Cargill, Inc.*, 445 F. Supp. 714, 721-22 (S.D.N.Y. 1978).

Once it is determined when the plaintiff was on notice of the fraudulent transfer or obligation (a/k/a the "discovery" date), then if suit was filed more than four (or five, or six) years after the date of the transfer or obligation, but within one (or two) years after the discovery date, then the statute of limitations for an intentional fraudulent transfer claim will not expire until the expiration of the one (or two) year period after the discovery date, referred to as the "tolling period." This means that if the plaintiff learns of the transfer or obligation within the original four (or five, or six) year limitations period, then the one (or two) year tolling period will extend the date by which suit must be filed beyond the original four (or five, or six) year limitations period, only if the discovery date occurred sometime after the first day of year three (or year four) following the date of the transfer or obligation. If the plaintiff does not discover the transfer or obligation until after the four (or five, or six) year limitations period has expired, then suit must be filed within one (or two) years after the discovery date.

The party seeking to toll the statute of limitations bears the burden of establishing that he could not, with reasonable diligence, have discovered the fraudulent transfer within the limitations period. *E.g.*, *Sabatino v. Galati*, 43 A.D. 3d 1136 (N.Y. App. Div. 2007); *Ehrler v. Cataffo*, 42 A.D. 3d 424 (N.Y. App. Div. 2007). What constitutes sufficient "notice" to the claimant to begin the running of the tolling period can be murky and is very fact specific. Counsel and clients should be prepared to take discovery and/or submit affidavits and supporting documentation on the discovery date issue, if suit is commenced outside the original four (or five, or six) year limitations period and be prepared for a fight. And again, this tolling analysis applies only to claims for intentional, not constructive, fraudulent transfers. No equitable tolling of the statute of limitations is available for constructive fraudulent transfer claims.

6.

More on the bar against constructive fraudulent transfer claims in § 546(e) of the Bankruptcy Code – *Tronox v. Kerr-McGee.*

Chapter 17 of the original *Fraudulent Transfer Handbook* discussed the defense to constructive fraudulent transfer claims contained in § 546(e) of the Bankruptcy Code, for transfers that fit the Bankruptcy Code's definition of "margin payments" or "settlement payments" made to certain parties. Forte, Earl M., *The Fraudulent Transfer Handbook* (2013 Ed.) at 100-02. Prior Chapter 17 also discusses the broad and liberal application that courts have given to the § 546(e) defense. *Id.* at 101-02. While acknowledging this broad and liberal application, the recent decision of the United States Bankruptcy Court for the Southern District of New York in *Tronox, Inc., et al. v. Kerr-*

McGee Corp., et al., 503 B.R. at 340-43 ("*Tronox*") (discussed above in chapter 2 with respect to other issues) concluded that the defendants in that case could not rely on a § 546(e) defense. In reaching its decision, the court in *Tronox* specified clearly the requirements for asserting a § 546(e) defense, laying out a useful checklist for practitioners in the process.

In *Tronox* the defendants argued that § 546(e) provided them with a complete defense to the plaintiff's constructive fraudulent transfer claims relating to Kerr-McGee's corporate restructuring plan because the transfers at issue were either "settlement payments" or payments made by or for the benefit of a "financial participant" in connection with a "securities contract." *Tronox*, 503 B.R. at 338. The court addressed the defendants' argument in the context of their motion for leave to amend their answer to plead a § 546(e) defense. *Id.* at 340-41.

The New York bankruptcy court began its analysis by first trying to determine whether the transfers at issue involved "settlement payments" within the definition of that term set forth in § 741(8) of the Bankruptcy Code. The court noted the difficulty in applying this definition, but concluded that "one clear condition is that the term must be viewed 'in the context of the securities trade'. . .where the 'parties use intermediaries to make trades of public stock, which are instantaneously credited, but in which the actual exchange of stock and consideration therefor takes place at a later date.'" *Id.* at 341 *citing Enron Creditors Recovery Corp. v. Alfa S.A.B. de C.V.*, 651 F. 3d 329, 334 (2d Cir. 2011); *Zahn v. Yucaipa Capital Fund*, 218 B.R. 656, 675 (D.R.I. 1998); *In re Kaiser Steel Corp.*, 952 F.2d 1230, 1237 (10th Cir. 1991).

The court in *Tronox* next analyzed the transactions at issue and concluded that while the settlement of a securities transaction had occurred as part of the final distribution of Tronox stock by Kerr-McGee, the specific cash distributions that were being challenged as fraudulent transfers by the plaintiff, were only "one-way" intercompany transfers of cash and were not "settlement payments" made in exchange for securities. *Tronox*, 503 B.R. at 341 *citing In re Appleseed's Intermediate Holdings, LLC*, 470 B.R. at 302; *see also In re Integra Realty Res., Inc.*, 198 B.R. 352, 360 (Bankr. D. Colo. 1996). The court further noted that the defendants had also failed to identify a "securities contract" involved with the transfers, as that phrase is commonly understood in the securities trade. On that basis, the court in *Tronox* did not permit the defendants to rely on a § 546(e) defense. *Tronox*, 503 B.R. at 343.

Based on *Tronox* and other leading cases on the subject (*e.g. Lowenschuss, etc. v. Resorts International, Inc. (In re Resorts International, Inc.)*, 181 F.3d 505 (3d Cir. 1999); *Enron Creditors Recovery Corp. v. Alfa S.A.B. de C.V.*, 651 F.3d 329), to successfully raise a § 546(e) defense to a constructive fraudulent transfer claim, the defendant must be able to prove: (1) the existence of a "securities contract," as that term is commonly understood in the securities trade; (2) that the transfers the plaintiff seeks to recover as fraudulent transfers were made pursuant to that "securities contract"; and (3) that the transfers the plaintiff seeks to recover as fraudulent transfers were made in exchange for "securities," as that word is commonly understood in the securities trade. *See also Grede v. FCStone*, 2014 WL 1041736 (7th Cir. 2014) (In ruling that pre and post-petition cash transfers made from an investment management firm Sentinel Management Group, Inc., to a futures commission merchant FCStone, LLC, were protected from avoidance as constructive fraudulent transfers by § 546(e), the court noted the broad language and application of the § 546(e) defense, but emphasized that a "settlement payment," as defined in § 741(8) of the Bankruptcy Code, must involve the payment of money in exchange for a security pursuant to a "securities contract.")

Thus, while the overall transactions at issue in *Tronox* involved securities, because there was no factual link between the transfers the plaintiff was seeking to recover as fraudulent transfers and the purchase or sale of a security pursuant to a "securities contract," the court concluded that the specific transfers at issue were simply "one-way" intercompany transfers of cash and would not allow the defendants to rely upon a § 546(e) "safe harbor" defense. *Tronox*, 503 B.R. at 341-43. *See also In re Appleseed's Intermediate Holdings, LLC*, 470 B.R. at 302.

Thus, while the § 546(e) defense remains very broad and liberally construed, *Tronox* makes clear that a defendant must satisfy minimum requirements to rely upon it – the transfers that the plaintiff seeks to recover as constructive fraudulent transfers must have been transfers made pursuant to a "securities contract" and must have been made in exchange for "securities," as those terms are commonly understood in the securities trade.

TABLE OF AUTHORITIES

CASES

Childs v. Brandon,
    90 A.D.2d 983 (N.Y. App. Div. 4th Dep't. 1982).............. 37

Citicorp Trust Bank, FSB v. Makkar, et al.,
    67 A.D. 3d 950 (N.Y. App. Div. 2d Dept. 2009) 38

Ehrler v. Cataffo,
    42 A.D. 3d 424 (N.Y. App. Div. 2007) 37, 39

Enron Creditors Recovery Corp. v. Alfa S.A.B. de C.V.,
    651 F. 3d 329 (2d Cir. 2011) 43, 44

Executive Benefits Insurance Agency, Petitioner v. Peter H. Arkison, Chapter 7 Trustee of the Estate of Bellingham Insurance Agency, Inc.,
    573 U.S. ___, 2014 WL 2560461 (2014).......... 7 and *passim*

Executive Benefits Insurance Agency v. Arkison (In the Matter of Bellingham Insurance Agency, Inc.),
    702 F. 3d 553 (9th Cir. 2012) 9, 10, 11

Granfinanciera, S.A. v. Nordberg,
    492 U.S. 33 (1989)... 8 and *passim*

Grede v. FCStone,
    2014 WL 1041736 (7th Cir. 2014) 44

In re Bennett Funding Group, Inc.,
    367 B.R. 302 (Bankr. N.D. N.Y. 2007).......................... 38

In re Braus,
    248 F. 55 (2d Cir. 1917) 20

In re Duncan & Forbes Dev., Inc.,
    368 B.R. 27 (Bankr. C.D. Cal. 2006) 21

In re Equipment Acquisition Resources, Inc.,
    742 F. 3d 743 (7th Cir. 2014) 32-34

In re Integra Realty Res., Inc.,
    198 B.R. 352 (Bankr. D. Colo. 1996) 43

In re Kaiser Steel Corp.,
    952 F.2d 1230 (10th Cir. 1991) 43

Lavin v. Kaufman,
    226 A.D. 2d 107 (N.Y. App. Div. 1996) 38

Level 3 Communications, Inc. v. Federal Insurance Company,
    272 F. 3d 908 (7th Cir. 2001) 27, 28, 31

Lowenschuss, etc. v. Resorts International, Inc. (In re Resorts International, Inc.),
    181 F.3d 505 (3d Cir. 1999) 43

Marshall v. Stern,
    600 F. 3d 1037 (9th Cir. 2010) 11

Michaelson v. Farmer, et al. (In re Appleseed's Intermediate Holdings, LLC),
    470 B.R. 289 (D. Del. 2012) 24-27

Michaelson v. Golden Gate Private Equity, Inc., et al. (In re Appleseed's Intermediate Holdings, LLC),
    2011 WL 6293251 (D. Del. 2011) 30

Michaelson v. Golden Gate Private Equity, Inc., et al.,
    Case No. 11-51847 (Bankr. Del. 2011) 24-27

Miller v. Polow, et al.,
    14 A.D.3d 368 (N.Y. App. Div. 2005) 37

Northern Pipeline Construction Co. v. Marathon Pipe Line Co.,
    458 U.S. 50 (1984) 8-11

Orchard Brands TopCo, LLC, et al. v. Twin Cities Fire Insurance Company, et al., Case No. CGC-12-526950, Statement of Decision – Phase I, Bifurcated Trial (January 24, 2014) 24-31

Sabatino v. Galati,
    43 A.D. 3d 1136 (N.Y. App. Div. 2007) 39

Sargiss v. Magarelli,
    50 A.D. 3d 1117 (N.Y. App. Div. 2008) 37

Shapiro v. Wilgus,
    287 U.S. 348, 53 S.Ct. 142, 77 L.Ed. 355 (1932) 21

Stanley v. U.S. Bank, N.A. (In re TransTexas Gas Corp.),
    597 F. 3d 298 (5th Cir. 2010) 27, 28, 31

Stern v. Marshall,
    131 S. Ct. 2594 (2011) 7-16

The Government of India and The Food Corporation of India v. Cargill, Inc.,
    445 F. Supp. 714 (S.D.N.Y. 1978) 38

Tronox, Inc., et al. v. Kerr-McGee Corp., et al.,
    503 B.R. 239 (Bankr. S.D.N.Y. 2013) 19-21, 41-45

Zahn v. Yucaipa Capital Fund,
 218 B.R. 656 (D.R.I. 1998) 43

STATUTES

California Uniform Fraudulent Transfer Act, Cal. Civ.
 Code § 3439, *et seq.* .... *passim*

Constitution of the United States, Art. III .... 10 and *passim*

Delaware Uniform Fraudulent Transfer Act, 6 Del. C.
 § 1301, *et seq.* .... *passim*

Massachusetts Uniform Fraudulent Transfer Act,
 Massachusetts General Law ch. 109A .... *passim*

New York Debtor and Creditor Law, § 270, *et seq.* .... *passim*

Pennsylvania Uniform Fraudulent Transfer Act, 12 Pa.
 C.S. § 5101, *et seq.* .... *passim*

Uniform Fraudulent Conveyance Act .... 18 and *passim*

Uniform Fraudulent Transfer Act .... 18 and *pasasim*

United States Bankruptcy Code,
 11 U.S.C. § 101, *et seq.* .... 18 and *passim*

United States Judiciary Act, 28 U.S.C. § 1, *et seq.* .... *passim*

Various state statutes of limitation 36

OTHER AUTHORITIES

Fed. R. App. Pro. 6 17

Forte, Earl M., *The Fraudulent Transfer Handbook*
 (2013 Ed.) .... 19 and *passim*

Rendleman, Doug, *Measurement of Restitution: Coordinating Restitution with Compensatory Damages and Punitive Damages*, 68 Washington & Lee L. Rev. 973 (2011).. 31, n.6

INDEX

"core" bankruptcy matters, 2, 8, 10, 12
"strong arm" power, 33
§ 546(e) of the Bankruptcy Code, 5, 6, 41
1984 bankruptcy amendments, 13
acts of fraud and acts of delay or hindrance, 20
actual intent to defraud creditors, 18
Anadarko Petroleum, 21
appeal, 11
Arch Insurance Company, 24
Article III of the Constitution, 2, 8
badges of fraud, 18, 19, 21
bifurcated, 24
California insurance law, 26
cash payments, 27, 29
Catlin Specialty Insurance Company, 24
certiorari, 12, 29
circumstantial evidence, 18
consent of the parties, 3, 8, 15
constitutional limits, 2, 6, 7, 11, 16

constructive fraudulent transfer, 36
constructive fraudulent transfers, 25, 35, 44, 45
core/non-core distinction, 14
Court of Appeals for the Seventh Circuit, 4, 32
coverage, 3, 6, 23, 24, 26, 28, 30
D&O, 3, 6, 23, 24, 25, 26, 28, 31
D&O insurance carriers, 24
de novo review, 2, 10, 12, 13, 14, 15, 16
defense costs, 23
Delaware court, 27
Delaware UFTA, 25
delayed, 19, 20
dilemma, 12
directors and officers, 3, 23, 28
disgorgement, 4, 26, 27
district court, 2, 9, 10, 11, 12, 13, 14, 15, 16, 25, 27, 29, 30, 33, 34
dividends, 25, 27
EBIA, 9, 10, 11, 12, 15
entry of final judgment, 2, 10, 12, 13, 15, 17

Equipment Acquisition Resources, 4, 32, 47
equitable "restitution", 28
equitable claim, 29, 30
equitable tolling, 5, 35, 36, 37
Executive Benefits, 2, 6, 7, 8, 9, 10, 11, 12, 13, 14, 15, 16, 46
Executive Benefits Insurance Agency v. Arkison (In the Matter of Bellingham Insurance Agency, Inc.), 9, 46
Executive Benefits Insurance Agency, Petitioner v. Peter H. Arkison, 7, 46
Fed. R. App. Pro. 6, 17, 49
federal judicial power, 8, 14
Fifth Circuit, 27
final judgments, 2, 7, 15
financial participant, 42
Forte, Earl M., 19, 23, 28, 36, 41
fraudulent transfer, 1, 2, 3, 4, 5, 6, 7, 9, 10, 12, 20, 23, 24, 25, 26, 28, 29, 30, 31, 33, 34, 35, 36, 37, 38, 39, 41, 42, 44
Fraudulent Transfer Handbook (2013 Ed.), 3, 4, 5, 18, 23, 28, 35, 36, 41, 49
Golden Gate Private Equity, Inc., 24, 30, 47, 48
Granfinanciera, 8, 9, 11, 28, 29, 30, 31, 46
Great American Insurance Company, 24
hindered, 19, 20
hindrance, 19
ill-gotten gain, 27
Illinois law, 33
in exchange for a security, 44
inquiry notice, 38
insurable "loss", 4, 26, 28, 31
insurance, 3, 6, 23, 24, 25, 26, 28, 30, 31
intent to defraud creditors can be inferred, 18
intentional fraudulent transfers, 19, 20, 36
IRS, 4, 5, 6, 32, 33, 34
judicial powers, 3, 8, 15
Judiciary Act, 2, 8, 10, 12, 13, 49
jury demand, 11, 29
jury trial, 11, 25, 29, 30
Kerr-McGee, 3, 5, 6, 18, 19, 20, 21, 41, 42, 43, 48
lack life tenure, 12, 14

lack of life tenure, 8, 11
legal claims, 4, 28, 29, 31
Level 3, 27, 28, 31, 47
Level 3 Communications, Inc. v. Federal Insurance Company, 27, 47
liability insurance coverage, 23
life tenure, 8
limitations periods, 5, 35, 36
liquidating trust, 25
margin payments, 41
Marshall v. Stern, 11, 47
Marshall v. Stern, 600 F. 3d 1037 (9th Cir. 2010), 11
Michaelson, 24, 25, 26, 27, 30, 47, 48
Michaelson v. Farmer, 24, 25
Ninth Circuit, 9, 10, 11, 12
no diminution, 8
non-core matters, 8
Northern Pipeline, 8, 9, 10, 11, 48
not an insurable "loss" under a D&O policy, 28
not insurable, 27
notice of the fraud, 38
one-year equitable tolling period, 36

Orchard Brands TopCo, LLC, 3, 6, 23, 24, 48
powers of bankruptcy judges, 2, 6, 7, 16
practical problem, 2, 8, 15
Practitioners, 16, 31
proof of claim, 28, 29
proposed findings of fact and conclusions of law, 2, 10, 13, 14, 16
reach back, 35
restitution, 4, 26, 28, 29, 31
safe harbor, 45
salary protection, 8, 11, 12, 14
securities contract, 42, 43, 44, 45
securities trade, 43, 44, 45
separability provision, 13
settlement payments, 41, 42, 43
Seventh Circuit, 27, 33, 34
six-year statute of limitations, 37
sovereign immunity, 33
Stanley v. U.S. Bank, N.A., 27, 48
statutes of limitations, 5, 35, 36
Stern, 2, 7, 9, 11, 12, 13, 14, 15, 16, 48
Stern claims, 2, 8, 10, 13

Stern v. Marshall, 2, 7, 48
Superior Court for the County of San Francisco, California, 24
Supreme Court of the United States, 2, 4, 7, 28, 55
Supreme Court opinion, 28
tax payments, 5, 32, 34
the bankruptcy reference, 11, 30
toll the statute of limitations, 39
TransTexas, 27, 28, 31, 48
Tronox, 3, 5, 6, 18, 19, 20, 21, 41, 42, 43, 44, 45, 48
trustee, 4, 9, 20, 25, 26, 27, 28, 29, 31, 32, 33, 34
Twin Cities, 3, 4, 6, 23, 24, 26, 27, 48
two year tolling period, 39
U.S. Specialty Insurance Company, 24
unconstitutional, 14
Uniform Fraudulent Conveyance Act, 18
Uniform Fraudulent Transfer Act, 18
United States Bankruptcy Code, 18, 49, 55
United States Bankruptcy Court for the Southern District of New York, 3, 5, 19, 41
United States Court of Appeals for the Eleventh Circuit, 29
United States Court of Appeals for the Ninth Circuit, 9
United States District Court for the District of Delaware, 30
unsecured creditor, 33
voidable under applicable law, 33
waiver of sovereign immunity, 32, 33
We reserve that question for another day, 16
White and Williams LLP, 55

About the Author

Earl M. Forte ("Fort") is a partner at the national law firm of Gordon Rees Scully & Mansukhani LLP and is a member of the firm's Commercial Litigation practce group and its Bankruptcy Restructuring and Creditors Rights practice group. He has substantial experience in bankruptcy and other insolvency and business winddown matters, including in fraudulent transfer litigation. Mr. Forte has been practicing law enthusiastically for over 30 years and represents clients in a variety of industries and matters that arise in diverse transactions and business contexts. He works regularly on matters involving the United States Bankruptcy Code and related laws. This is the first supplement to Mr. Forte's first book, the *Fraudulent Transfer Handbook*, originally published in 2013 and re-issued in 2017. See www.amazon.com. More information about Mr. Forte's background and his law firm Gordon Rees is available at Gordon Rees's website www.grsm.com.

www.ingramcontent.com/pod-product-compliance
Lightning Source LLC
Chambersburg PA
CBHW050021230526
45470CB00003B/1077